Second-Class
PROFESSOR

SECOND-CLASS
PROFESSOR

Who is teaching our students?
What you need to know if you're
paying for college.

ANGELA HURD

authorHOUSE®

AuthorHouse™ LLC
1663 Liberty Drive
Bloomington, IN 47403
www.authorhouse.com
Phone: 1-800-839-8640

Published by AuthorHouse 04/07/2014

ISBN: 978-1-4969-0325-9 (sc)
ISBN: 978-1-4969-0326-6 (e)

CONTENTS

Last semester a 40-year old college student of mine approached me after finals week to give me a "Thank You" card. Although she knew she had earned a "C" in the class, she wanted to thank me for, in her words, "teaching me how to think." As she was saying goodbye she cryptically stated that God told her I should write a book. I blushed and said I had already written one that no one wanted to publish. She just shrugged and sweetly encouraged me to do it. This is not the book I had previously written. This is a horror story, or a comedy.

Today I am waiting to find out if I will be teaching a college course which will take place 12 hours from now. I have taught this course before, but not for several years, and not at this college. If assigned this course along with the other class that I have prepared, I will need to have a syllabus ready by tomorrow. I will only be informed by e-mail if this course is to be mine to teach, and sometimes there have been problems with the e-mail system at this college. I pace and chew my lip. I hate to be unprepared. Last night on the off-chance that I would be assigned this class, I got a colleague to forward his sample syllabus. He said that no text book was available for me yet, but that he would try to get one from the person who taught this class last summer. When that would be, I don't know.

My anxiety is rising, so I start to make a syllabus knowing that all my time could be wasted. I find an advertisement of the text online which happens to have the table of contents for the textbook. I use the chapter headings to make a reading schedule for students based on the topics covered and put assignments with the corresponding chapters. It turns out that putting together a course without a textbook is a bit tricky. At least I have something prepared.

To kill the time I mow the grass, fearful that I will miss an e-mail asking me to teach the course. The last time that I didn't respond right away, the course was given to someone else. I mow for 15 minutes, run inside, check e-mail; repeat. Since no message has been forthcoming, I will just write down the saga of my masochistic attachment to life as an adjunct college instructor. An adjunct is "temporary," but often full-time for years; a professor who has no office but actually teaches a full-time schedule. These instructors bear the same demands as full-time college professors.

As I was writing the above paragraph I heard a chime from my e-mailbox with this statement. "Mr. Jones has decided that to teach that class. Sorry to have dangled a possibility that didn't materialize."

Just for the record, "Mr. Jones" is a full-time professor who does exactly the same thing as I do for more pay, health benefits, sick and vacation time, job security via tenure, and his pick of the classes. It is not his fault that he has scored a full-time position, and I have nothing against this person. However, I have endured no end of inconveniences in order to do what I love, and I am not alone. What follows is not a bitter diatribe listing my personal grievances. **This will be a discussion of how higher education is doing a disservice to both educators and students by treating the adjuncts, who teach a majority of college students in the US, as second-class citizens.**

As I discuss the national trend to move most college education to adjunct teachers, I will weave in my story along with the stories of my adjunct colleagues. I will explain how that effects those paying for college, and I will do so in the following chapters:

Before publishing this book, I showed it to a few colleagues. They all said this message needed to get out to the public. They also thought it may be the end of my teaching career because my school would not be pleased with my honesty. I shelved the book for 3 months, wondering what to do. Then I read Sheryl Sandberg's book, "Lean In: Women, Work and the Will to Lead." I was inspired by the poster on the wall at Google where she trained other leaders. It read, "What would you do if you weren't afraid." Well, I'm still afraid, but I want to start a dialogue which will improve the way our college students are educated, so here it is.

FOREWORD

---•❧•---

Second-Class Professor addresses the challenges of higher education head on in a compelling, no-holds-barred look at the employment of adjunct professors. This book observes the life of an adjunct professor: receiving your course information the day before term begins, operating out of your trunk, praying for a desk to sit at and a printer to use. It examines the impact of the adjunct's treatment on the quality of education students receive, and offers practical ways to improve the overall educational experience for both staff and student. From the personal standpoint to the big picture perspective, Angela Hurd takes you inside the walls of higher education as you may have never experienced it before!

Rebecca Hart, Co-Pastor, Liberty Presbyterian Church

CHAPTER I

The Reason Adjuncts Are Used or,
Would You Mind Working With No Contract
for 2 Weeks and for Free For 4 Weeks?

According to Audrey Williams June's article in the *Chronicle of Higher Education*, 70% of all college professors are of adjunct status. Eighty five percent of community college professors are adjuncts.[1] So, what exactly defines an adjunct and why are they so popular? *Webster's Dictionary* defines adjunct as something "subordinate" or "temporary," yet most of us really have no real direct supervision at all, so who are we subordinate to? Most have taught full-time for years, so we really aren't temporary. In reality, adjuncts have been hired to teach the main load of classes at most colleges and universities so that the few tenured faculty can devote their time to research. Therefore, the adjuncts focus on teaching, and the establishment only pays a few professors living wages with benefits. An adjunct is hired for one course at a time and does not receive any health benefits, sick or vacation time. All-in-all, it is a great deal for the institution. The actual person who has the most contact with the paying student has no voice, and no job security, which I will discuss further in this chapter.

As I was submitting this book to my editor in February of 2014, I caught a news report about the faculty on strike at the University of Illinois in Chicago. These were full-time non-tenured faculty striking for better pay and benefits. I'm sure they have some valid grievances and deserve better pay, but these professors are earning a regular salary! An adjunct who is teaching a majority of the college classes at most colleges and universities is paid even less and has less job security than those on strike in Chicago. I feel a revolution coming in higher education. The huge disparity between the way a tenured professor and an adjunct is treated is even greater than the two parties involved in the conflict in Chicago.

Thanks to President Obama's health plan, those working 30 hours per week now must receive health benefits. However, colleges and universities get around that by policing their adjuncts, insuring that no one works near 30 hours. Because every hour in the classroom represents nearly 3 hours of prep time and grading, the college has indicated that 11 hours of classes represents close to 30 hours of work. I tutor as well as teach, and I have to clock in to two different websites before seeing a student in the tutoring center. This is the college's way of making sure I don't get near the 30-hour mark. An article in the *Huffington Post* by Tyler Kinkade quotes an American Association of University Professor as stating "Such actions are reprehensible, penalizing part-time faculty members both by depriving them access to affordable health care as intended by law and by reducing their income."[2] Apparently, the AAUP's statements have no clout in actual teaching institutions.

Most of my colleagues have cobbled together a living by teaching at two or three different colleges in the same city, but heaven help them if they get sick with no health benefits. This shuttling between several schools works when an adjunct has transportation, and lives in a city large enough to have several institutions nearby, but isn't possible for adjuncts teaching in areas with only one university in a specific region.

According to the Bureau of Labor Statistics, an adjunct working full-time makes less than one-third of what a full-time professor makes, even though the education required is exactly the same in most schools. Given that 70-85% of all college teachers are adjuncts, that saves each school a great deal of money. These adjuncts also don't get an office, and may, or may not have one lounge/computer to share with other adjuncts. Facility savings alone make for millions of dollars in funds and I will discuss the facility issue more in chapter five. In researching this salary information, I discovered that even among other adjuncts, the college where I teach pays one of the lowest amounts per class. However, I continued to punish myself by doing more research, and this is what I learned.

The liability faced by the academic institution is also lessened by the use of adjuncts because an adjunct can't sue for a breach of contract, or unsafe working conditions. Of course, this also saves each school millions. I will discuss the actual physical dangers of being an adjunct in chapter 8 which I have titled, "Safety issues and blood in the hallway, or should I risk my life for this when I don't get disability insurance?"

There are some types of jobs that require one to put in a month of work before ever receiving payment for the work performed. No matter what job this is, at the beginning of the cycle, it is a long wait for that first check. Physicians, therapists, social workers, and anyone else who bills insurance and waits to be reimbursed will not be paid for actual work performed for months. They may have to make numerous phone calls to insurance processing representatives in order to get paid. I have heard these complaints reported in the media and I sympathize with these professionals. I understand that many careers work that way. Even farmers must wait a while to recoup their investments.

An adjunct at my college will begin planning a course weeks before teaching, making lesson plans, maybe writing tests or preparing PowerPoint presentations. Then, they will teach for 2 weeks before even receiving a contract indicating that they will be paid at all! A class can be cancelled or given to another teacher up until the day before it meets for the first time. Reasons for cancelling a class include: the enrollment falls below a certain number set by the institution, a full-timer has taken a fancy to that class and now wants it, or your department chair is in a bad mood. All your preparation time is lost, and you will not be compensated for it. Any complaining on your part will indicate that you are a whiner, and your department chair will be less willing to assign you a class next semester. Biting your tongue is the number one physical exercise performed by most adjuncts. The powerlessness of adjuncts allows department chairs to get away with all kinds of abuse.

So, we have established that despite the rising cost in a college degree, the actual teaching institutions have found a way to save at least one-third of the cost of the average professor's salary. Adjuncts really are quite a good bargain for their employer.

However, for some of you who are reading this book as a student paying for college, a taxpayer wondering how the state is using your dollars, or a parent hoping their investment is going to their child's education, you should know about how much money is going to the people who actually pass or fail a student. The people who are giving students life skills and credentials to start a successful career are at the bottom of the pay scale at a most colleges and universities nation-wide. Building maintenance employees at most of these schools make much more money, have a secure and dependable work schedule, and have full benefits, where the adjuncts do not. Wow, I AM a good bargain!

CHAPTER II

Adjuncts at 4-year Colleges vs. 2-year, or
How Many Types of Learning Disabilities
Can You Teach at the College Level?

I have taught as an adjunct at three different four-year universities and two different two-year community colleges in three different states. This has given me a very broad look at the different ways an adjunct can be used. One of the 4-year universities was a small liberal arts school; one was a for-profit business school, while the other was a large state school. In general, students at a school that screens its students and has high standards for acceptance, will have easier students to teach. While teaching at two of the 4-year schools, I found the students to be prepared for learning. The for-profit business school was lenient and encouraged less-prepared students to take classes. One could surmise that this was to increase revenue, but more on the business school later.

At 4-year schools with a graduate program in an adjunct's field of study, the need for adjuncts is limited because the college will use graduate students to teach introductory courses. The only reason I was added to the faculty of the liberal arts school is because someone in the four-member department suddenly died and the Dean knew of my work at the local community college. My husband and I used to joke that "Someone will have to die at _____college before another teacher is hired." We were stunned that it actually happened, but I was grateful for the job.

I was thankful for the increase in salary at the liberal arts school, and I found that was the most lucrative adjunct gig in my life. The campus was lovely, and for the most part, I enjoyed teaching there. Students at this school had to have a relatively high GPA and most had good skills. However, it was considered the school for the rich kids, as it was an expensive school, and some students were spoiled. Some went as far as to threaten to have their parents "talk" to me if I gave them a bad grade. Some of these kids had been coasting and were not used to working hard. I am not easy to intimidate, and I handed out the grades students had earned just as I had been doing for 10 years. The reason I say "kids" is because at two of the 4-year schools the students were of a traditional age for the most part. Students were mostly between 18 and 25.

Being an adjunct at the 4-year business school taught me about the politics of a for-profit school. The students at this school were working full time and most classes were in the evenings. I taught mainly junior-level business writing classes and I was hired for my "real world" experience as well as years teaching. I had worked in sales and in human resources for a government contractor to the Department of Labor. This experience made me valuable to the business school.

The accelerated course that I taught at the business school met for 8 weeks only. Everything was standardized by the department, and I had already graded one paper and was returning it on the first day that I met the class. Students had accessed online information and were to write a simple paper in APA writing style. As this was a business writing course, I was shocked that over half the class didn't know how to write in APA style. Using the standardized rubric for the class, I had to fail these students. Imagine walking in to face your class for the first time knowing that they had already seen their bad grade posted on the online grade book. It was not pleasant!

I started class with, "I know many of you are disappointed in your grade, for this Junior-level course. Let me start by asking how many of you have taken the pre-requisite course, or the one required before this one?" Less than half the hands were raised. No wonder they all did so poorly! I encouraged them to take the previous course instead in order to have a successful experience. Of course, none did because registration had let them in to this course. If they could just pass it, they would save money!

I decided to give the class a quick reminder of the basics of the previous course for about 1 hour. I then offered to re-grade their first paper. It took days to re-grade, but I felt that if registration had made a mistake, I should try to help the students. After my boss and I did some digging, we discovered that it was now the school's policy not to enforce pre-requisites. Their reason? The competing for-profit college next door had stopped enforcing theirs. This put me in a terrible position. I could not, in good conscience, be a part of this. I would not inflate grades, so I knew I would have to fail a lot of students. Being an adjunct, I had no voice, or contract, so after I finished this term, I left for the community college next door.

Stuart Rojstaczer and Christoper Healy's article, "Grading in American Colleges and Universities," shows that grades increased over a 15-year period at 4-year colleges, while they did not increase at community colleges.[3] Grade inflation, however, was the worst at private schools. Perhaps these colleges feel more pressure to prove their worth and that causes them to pressure teachers to give higher grades. I certainly can attest to that after my experience at two different types of private schools.

To further support my concerns about grade inflation, an article by Allysia Finley in August 24th 2013's <u>Wall Street Journal</u>, quoted a well-known economics professor. Finley interviewed 72 year-old Richard Veddar who has taught economics since 1965. In his discussion of the increased cost of a college education he states, "I can tell you right now, having taught at universities forever, that universities will do everything they can to get students to graduate. If you think we have grade inflation now, you ought to think that will happen. If you breathe into a mirror and it fogs up, you'll get an 'A'."[4]

To sum up the experience of being an adjunct at a 4-year college, I discovered the following:

-For-profit schools and private schools may pay an adjunct better.

-For-profit and private schools will pressure you to give good grades to justify their tuition prices.

-Four-year state schools have little need for adjuncts as they use less-prepared graduate students.

To cap off my adjunct experience at the four-year-for-profit business school, I was bullied by one of my students and pressured to pass him. He said, "You are the only teacher here to give me these grades." He was one of the students who had not taken the prerequisite writing class and could not write in the required APA writing style. He stayed after class each night speaking angrily, getting very close to me, and would not let me show him how to improve. I tried to encourage him to drop and take the previous course. He refused. His last paper was surprisingly written. It was quite professional, and devoid of all his trademark mistakes. I knew right away that he had not written it, and that it had been purchased from a writing service. In fact, it was written using an ancient footnoting method. I failed him on the paper because it was not written in APA style which was required by my department, and he failed the course as well. He promptly got a lawyer, and called a meeting with my Dean claiming I failed him because he was from Turkey. My boss called me and after listening to my story said I didn't have to prove he had not written his last paper, the fact that it wasn't in APA format was enough to fail a student. This took 2 months to sort out after I was done teaching the class. So, my thankless chore of trying to teach concepts from the first course and re-grading the first papers for this class was met with a discrimination accusation. It seemed that going back to the community college next door was a good idea.

My experience working at two community colleges in different parts of the country is, of course, you won't be teaching any junior or senior-level courses. There may only be 3 different introductory courses in an adjunct's department, which can get repetitive. One of the biggest complications as a teacher at a community college is that the school is open to anyone who can pay or get financial aid, which means everyone. The community college where I currently work provides remedial courses in every subject to teach students the skills they may have missed in high school.

What this means in a practical sense, is that by the time a student makes it to my introductory course, he/she may have taken classes for a year at the college already getting prepared for my class. This system works great, unless grade inflation, or student cheating, plagues a teacher in the introductory course. I had a student who was struggling with in-class written work, yet did well on papers prepared outside of class. He finally admitted to me that his mother wrote the papers making passing grades. I suspected something was going on, so I increased the amount of in-class writing the students had to produce. There was no way I was going to prove his mother wrote the papers if he contested his grade to the Department Chair, and I needed to fail this student. I didn't want to be the one to pass him on to another teacher knowing he did not have passing writing skills! My system worked. Especially when I made the final exam an in-class essay exam. Discovering this deception, and taking care of it took a lot of time and creativity on my part. It is easy to see how less-motivated teachers can let a student pass in this situation.

As I described in the grade-inflation article, 2-year colleges are less prone to grade inflation. Perhaps this is because we always deal with under-prepared students and are not afraid to give accurate grades. It may also be because our students feed into 4-year schools who will only accept our student's transfer credits if they feel our school truly prepares students.

As the title of this chapter indicates, I have had to teach students with a large variety of learning disabilities. My community college tests students and identifies which disabilities they have and directs them to remedial courses. This doesn't mean that I have academically prepared students in my classes, however. As discussed previously, students can cheat in a writing course, having another person write their papers so they can get into a freshman or sophomore-level class. When this happens you can have a person in your class who can't pass 8th-grade English sitting next to a four-year student who is taking a class at the community college to save money. I have had students in my classes who already have Master's degrees, but need my class for a specific certification. I also had a student who tested at a 1st or 2nd-grade reading level and whose disability included "troubles with comprehension." This person could not read the text, could not understand case studies or test questions, and could not participate in group work.

Short of the one-room-schoolhouse, there are not many teaching environments with such ability differences. The one-room-schoolhouse has the advantage of teaching a lower academic level to lower grades. An adjunct at a community college with no barriers to entry must teach whoever pays to get into the class. Speaking of payment; the student with the primary-school reading-level was receiving financial aid to take a class that he had no chance of passing. Frankly, he looked shell-shocked in class and confessed that he "had no idea what was going on." Other students begged me not to put him in their group for projects, and I tried to encourage him to take the pre-requisite course again and withdraw so he could get his money back. He declined. Perhaps because he wasn't paying to take the class in the first place, he wasn't worried about failing and losing his money.

Because I have to fill out a Financial Aid attendance form to ensure students receiving aid are attending class, I discovered the student with this low reading level was receiving aid. At some point, it is unethical to collect payment from the state via financial aid for a student when they have no chance of success. This student may have found a few teachers to slip him past with a "C", but an instructor like myself would eventually fairly grade this student. I did some research on this student and called the Disability Center to see what his disability was and how he had gotten into my class. He had passed remedial English with a "C", and was being encouraged by his mother to get a degree. Apparently, he had done well in his classes in welding and mechanics. When I asked his counselor, "Who told him he should take my class and when they knew he had a 1st-grade reading level?" The counselor told me they don't advise a student, they just help them identify their disability.

Let's be clear here. Financial aid comes from all working adults. This aid comes from our federal and state taxes, and when used correctly will help society in the long run, but only if it is not wasted. Students who are pushed into classes where they cannot succeed drain the system and prevent them from completing a degree they can prosper in. I know that is the beauty of the 2-year college's open-enrollment policies, but it leads to a waste of taxpayer money. According to the Institute for College Access & Success, 83% of community college students had a documented need of financial aid in the 2007-2008 academic year. It would be great if that aid was given to students in areas where they had the likelihood of succeeding.

Another sad reality is that some students are using their financial aid to cover housing. If these students are not qualified to stay in college, they risk losing their room and board. I once had a student with a severe brain injury. She had suffered a horrible car crash and had neurological damage and had injured some internal organs. She had trouble following along in class, and when I spoke to her, she couldn't keep a train of thought. I told her I thought she was trying to go to college too soon. I advised her to drop out and give her body time to heal. She then shared that she was living with and taking care of her grandma who had mild dementia. According to the student, no other relative was willing to take care of her grandma, and both of them were living on the financial aid the student received. If she dropped out, both she and grandma would be on the street.

It is true that financial aid does cover some housing costs for students.[5] I don't doubt that what this girl told me was true, but I couldn't be responsible for these two lives. She was not passing the class. I told her that there had to be other social safety nets for them and advised her that I would grade her fairly. She earned a "D" in the class. On my teaching evaluation one student had stated that I was "heartless and discriminated against learning disabilities."

As stated above, it is wrong for a community college to use taxpayer money for these students who cannot pass a class, but it is also wrong to take money from students themselves for classes they cannot succeed in. Many of my students take four years to finish a two-year degree and each class costs them dearly. Parents are paying babysitters so they can attend class and working less so there is less money to operate their households. The system truly must change to ensure that the classes they take are appropriate and that they have a reasonable chance of passing.

A solution to this would be complex, but would involve some kind of advising. No one wants to kill someone's dream, but a good advisor could steer a student in the direction of success. One cringes to think of international communities which test students while they are young and pegs them for certain careers with little room for personal choice. Obviously that is the extreme we should avoid. However, we need a common-sense approach to guiding a student into a successful education and career. Telling a student that they can fulfill his or her dreams and be the anything if they work hard enough is NOT being truthful. What if I had the dream of playing in the WMBA? I am 5'3" with no aptitude for the sport of basketball. In fact, I grew up in Indiana where nearly everyone else played but me. I am naturally talented at other things, but would never have succeeded in basketball. If that was my dream and I worked hard at it, I would have become a mediocre high school player at best. I would not have felt successful, and I would never have taken up the hobbies where I have succeeded.

That is the saddest thing about open enrollment with little academic counseling. A gifted mechanic or musician will continue to take courses in which they have little aptitude and our schools will keep on taking tax payers' financial aid for these students. As long as a student, or the government can pay for a student to take a course, why should the college care if they succeed? The bottom line is that two-year colleges need to be accountable for the money they accept in aid for these students. If they were accountable, a student with a 1st grade reading level would not be able to use government aid to take a freshman-level English course.

CHAPTER III

Adjuncts Are Worse Than Scabs, or
My First Faculty Meeting

Imagine that it is 2006. I have just been interviewed and hired at a community college. The Academic Chair of the department who just hired me says, "We are having a faculty meeting in 10 minutes, why don't you join me." I follow him to a lecture hall and sit with a group of strangers from two similar disciplines, housed in one department. At least 80 percent of us in the room are adjuncts. As the meeting progresses it occurs to me that the full-time faculty at this college are on strike. How did I NOT know this? In my defense, I had just moved, I had two small children, and we were not getting the local newspaper. My daily National Public Radio listening must not have been enough to keep me informed.

Things were getting ugly in this meeting. At times, the full-time people would look around at the faculty near them and try to get a nod of support for their grievance. It seemed odd to me that the full-time folks seemed unaware that none of the benefits they were fighting over were offered to us. We had no dog in this fight at all. In fact, more classes were given to adjuncts to avoid having to hire another full-time potential striker! We essentially were like scabs crossing a picket line, working in their stead. In what other working environment are the strikers and scabs put together in regular meetings as if they are exactly the same?

In one way, at this 2-year school, we were and still are exactly the same. We do essentially the same job. Granted, some full professors serve in leadership or training positions, but I have rarely seen them, let alone received any teaching guidance from them. In fact, I have had full-timers come to my class to take notes so they could use some of my teaching strategies!

A few years ago, in Columbus Ohio, Governor Kasich introduced legislation that would limit the bargaining power of employees in a union. As members of a teacher's union, the tenured folks at my school protested daily. Full-timers in my department were organized and motivated to march and assemble at the capital. Some of these protesters were friends of mine who spoke about their feelings of solidarity and power and they invited me to join them. I know that some of these people had themselves started as adjuncts. How could they not see that I had no reason to join them when I was left out of the club!

Sarah Kendzior, Phd. wrote an article about adjuncts called "Academia's Indentured Servants."[6] The title alone speaks volumes. She writes, "On Twitter, I wondered why so many professors who study injustice ignore the plight of their peers. 'They don't consider us their peers,' the adjuncts wrote back. Academia likes to think of itself as a meritocracy—which it is not—and those who have tenured jobs like to think they deserved them. They probably do—but with hundreds of applications per available position, an awful lot of deserving candidates have defaulted to the adjunct track." Her observations seemed to mirror mine. She goes as far as to label academia as a "caste system," where most tenured faculty refuse to speak up for the plight of their colleagues.

Let me be clear here. I don't want to be a part of the teacher's union. I'm not pushing for health insurance for adjuncts because I know that is where the serious cost to the college lies, and at one point in my life, I wanted a flexible work schedule. What I want for myself and other proven adjuncts with the same amount of experience as most tenured faculty, is an income and a schedule that I can count on. I would like to know that I will be assigned 3 classes each semester. Not four classes one semester, and only one the next leaving me to find some other part-time filler. I know that enrollments change and sometimes enough classes are not available, but I personally have kept my teaching diverse so I can teach 4-5 different classes in order to be relevant in my department. If my employer was committed to giving me a certain number of classes, I would have far more job security, and I would feel more like a part of the academic team.

Kendzior also notes that some adjuncts have devoted so much time into their education that they will not pursue another career because it would mean giving up their goal. Some do work at other jobs, but doing so leaves them available to teach fewer classes. This indicates that you are not serious about being a tenure-track professor and may make it tougher to break in to a full-time position. Since 2008, colleges and universities have limited the number of full-time positions, even though the number of students has increased. The competition for a full-time position is now fiercer than ever.

Some colleges are trying to give their adjuncts a little of the respect they deserve. Universities in Iowa and Maryland are giving their experienced adjuncts "Adjunct Professor" status. As a college instructor does the exact work in the classroom as a tenured professor, it is only right that they be called "Professor" even if they add "Adjunct" as a prefix. These positions go to teachers who have taught at least 5 years and who have passed several evaluation markers. For this reason, for the rest of this book, I will refer to an adjunct instructor as an adjunct professor out of respect for the job.

The four-year-liberal arts college where I taught as an adjunct was starting to level the status of adjuncts to that of professors in a cosmetic way as well. They were allowing adjuncts to be described as "faculty" instead of merely, "staff." Seeing my college condescend to this wasn't really a reward for me. It just made sense. In any other academic setting, those who teach are "faculty". Those who work in administration or maintenance are "staff." The fact that it was considered a big deal for a college to use a word according to its rightful dictionary definition is telling. It is curious too, the way it provides for complexity when mass e-mails are sent. Anything my current college has to send out to all teachers can't be sent: "To all faculty, "it must say "To all faculty and staff." Then the sender has to have two list serves; one for real staff, and one for teaching staff which really get included on all faculty messages. Sound confusing? What if we just called anyone who teaches at the college level "faculty" and use the term correctly?

Quibbling over low-level titles may sound trivial. But imagine being a surgeon who just saved a patient's life. Now imagine that when an article is written about the patient's recovery, you are mentioned as a nurse who helped on the case. It is not that being a nurse is menial, it just denies your training and experience, not to mention tremendous work on behalf of this patient. Every e-mail I receive from my department which labels me as "staff" is a little reminder of my "less-than" status.

CHAPTER IV

Adjuncts and the Mobile Office, or
Do You Have a Stapler in that Briefcase?

An adjunct professor may or may not have access to office space. Where I currently teach, I do have one file cabinet drawer in which to put things for one of the four classes that I teach. Sometimes, I can actually use this storage space. However, this semester I am teaching at two different satellite locations. Sometimes I will teach two different classes on two different campuses. This brings me to the mobile office. Because none of the smaller campus locations provide any storage options for me, my car is my office. The back seat can have tests to copy, handouts and extra syllabi, etc.

I have become rather skilled at looking professional while going out to my car to root around for an old handout that a student needs. Sometimes I fib and say, "It's in my office, can I bring it for you Tuesday?" It is hard to keep forms/tests in good order when they are constantly moved to and from the car. I once saw a dog hair on a test I was handing a student. (I have 2 German Shepherds who sometimes ride in the back of the car.) I quickly switched tests with the student saying, "I think that one is missing a page."

We are not compensated for mileage when we must drive between campuses during the day. We cannot be late due to traffic, or our entire class section will be behind. I admit to some aggressive driving in order to make some of these classes.

I also teach on the main campus which does have one faculty work room. This room houses all the Biology, Science, English, and Communication Adjuncts. There are only six computers, one printer, and one refrigerator in this room. Oh, and a microwave that is so filthy I have never dared to warm my leftovers there. I run all the way across to another building for that. Granted, I do have access to my Communication Department's two adjunct desks, but my file cabinet is in another building, so I don't go there unless I need to warm up lunch. One poor soul never has scored a file cabinet drawer in the large combined workspace. He carries an 8 and 1/2" by 22" paper box around with him to class and back again, leaving it on top of a file cabinet. He is adept at balancing it on his shoulder when he walks to class through the crowded halls.

It is funny how many times I have been asked for a stapler by my students. It is obvious that I walk in with a brief case bulging with their graded papers. I also have to carry my own chalk because is seems to walk away from the classrooms and it is never there when I need it. If I am teaching in a room with a white board, I must carry my own dry-erase marker. Armed with only my briefcase, I would not have room for a stapler, yet students always ask. They seem to think that, not only do I have an office nearby, but that I carry it with me. Which is nearly true.

The over-crowded adjunct office with Biology, English, Science and Communications adjuncts is a fun and stimulating place. I love learning how other teachers handle cheating, poor attendance, and fire drills. This office can only be accessed by swiping my ID card. Last year, after teaching at this school for 8 years, my swipe card suddenly stopped working at the beginning of a new semester. I couldn't access my textbook for the courses, but I had my syllabi, so I got through the day. After some inquiries, I discovered that adjuncts are considered so temporary, that their keys are deactivated every single semester and must be reactivated once they have been assigned classes. There was barely 2 weeks between semesters, and I had been assigned 3 classes, yet I was shut out of my own office. I was told that I needed to fill out a new key request form even though I had been working there since 2005. I filled out the form. After 2 weeks of not being able to access my own file cabinet, I saw my department chair. "How can I teach when I've been shut off from my own teaching materials?" I asked. He got on the phone and magically the situation was resolved. Ironically, just this week the same thing has happened. Although I was on the main campus all summer, this fall, my key to my shared office space no longer works.

As you can see, it is not just the need to have a mobile office that makes an adjunct professor feel unappreciated. When we are given a single file drawer as a small convenience, we can be considered so temporary, that we are shut off from that convenience every 15 weeks.

This proved embarrassing when I had to pound on the door, hoping another faculty member was in the office. I needed to retrieve a test from my file drawer and I prayed someone would open so I would have time to copy it before class. Unfortunately, some students saw me and asked if I'd misplaced my key. I mumbled something non-committal. What could I say? I couldn't say that my employer had disabled my key! They would think I was a felon or something!

Obviously, treating 85% if your teaching staff unprofessionally is annoying to the adjunct faculty. But how does this affect students, or taxpayers funding a student through financial aid? A student—teacher relationship can effect a pupil's success greatly. Think about how many people have said they grew to hate a subject in high school because of a certain teacher. Also, think of how many young people go into a certain field because of a gifted, inspiring teacher. It would be great if every adjunct could be inspiring. It would be easier to be charismatic and prepared if I had a professional space that I could access, let alone call my own, store my things, and meet with students.

CHAPTER V

The Tenured vs. the Great Unwashed Masses.

The tenure system has been scoffed at for many years, and there has always been a gulf between the tenured, and un-tenured. However, there is a huge gap between an adjunct and both a tenured faculty member and a full-time professor seeking tenure.

I will list the differences and discuss each one:

1. Tenured/full time faculty cannot be fired, and an adjunct's job is at risk every 15 weeks.
2. Tenured/full-time faculty get the pick of the classes; adjuncts get the worst classes if any.
3. Tenured/full-time faculty earn sick leave and vacation pay and adjuncts do not.
4. Tenured/full-time faculty earn health, life, and disability insurance and adjuncts to not.
5. Tenured/full-time teachers have their name posted beside available courses so students who like them as an instructor can find which courses they are teaching; adjuncts do not.
6. Don't even get me started on sabbatical.

OK, we've already discussed how adjuncts don't get any benefits providing they work less than 30 hours. However, SOME of the full-timers where I have worked put in less than 30 hours, yet have a wonderful benefit package. Even the National Education Association states that "Part-time faculty are not unqualified, but they are exploited. Most part-time faculty earn very low 'per course' salaries and few, if any, benefits. The nature of their employment (many have a full-time job off campus) often does not enable them to advise students adequately, conduct research or contribute to the academic direction of the institution. A recent national survey indicates one half of part-time faculty do not hold office hours or meet with students outside the classroom."[7] This criticism of adjuncts not holding office hours by the NEA is laughable after my previous chapter describing how we have no offices! The fact that we are reachable 24/7 via e-mail helps us answer student questions no matter where we are. I agree that meeting one-on one with a student would be nice if I had a private office.

Perhaps the greatest disparity between adjunct professors and tenured or full professors is that many full-timers have grown complacent and aren't good teachers. I do know some who are, however, some don't do as good a job as the adjuncts. And why should they? They don't have to prove themselves every 15 weeks. They won't have one student complaint call their teaching into question. In fact, some are not accountable to anyone as far as I can see. I am not alone in this opinion. A study co-authored by Northwestern University president Morton Schapiro, a consultant named Kevin Soter and professor, David Figlio, confirms my position. Their article, "The Greatest Good" states that, "faculty who aren't on the tenure-track appear to do a better job than their tenured/ tenure-track peers when it comes to teaching freshmen undergraduates." According to their study, part-time teachers provided more inspiration and preparation to their students.

Having to prove myself every 15 weeks does make me work harder to prepare each class. In contrast to some of the full-time faculty where I work, I have worked in the "real world." I bring real-life examples to my teaching and my assignments are geared towards preparing students for this real world. I know tenured English professors who are so far behind on their grading that students can't improve their skills because they don't know what they did wrong on the first paper. Students complain bitterly that they would have not made the same mistakes on the 2nd and 3rd papers if they had gotten their first work graded and returned to them in time. Not only is this lazy technique preventing students from learning, it is blatant hypocrisy. How can we require students to turn their work in on time, if we don't return it in a timely way? If we are teaching students to be prepared for the world of work, we should be an example of a good employee.

I have had new full-time professors sit in on my business communication courses because they have not taught the course before and they want to see how I do it. Actually, they took a lot of notes so they could "borrow" my teaching ideas. I wouldn't mind training another employee if they weren't making 5 times what I was and getting ready to steal this class as soon as I was done with this 15-week section!

Having someone sit in on your class, takes notes, borrow your syllabus to get ideas and then bump you from that course so that you are never assigned it again is painful. However, it is not as painful as having a crazy person assigned classes over you! I have observed a tenured faculty member shriek and babble deranged accusations during several faculty meetings. This person is famous for her eccentricities. I once saw a disgusted student leaving this professor's class armed with her cell phone stating, "That's it, I'm showing this to the Dean. (She had taken a picture in class with her phone.) She taught us today using hand puppets! She's nuts and we aren't learning a thing!" This professor has continued to teach in our department for another 10 years and nothing seems to prevent her from being assigned classes, which I would gladly teach. To add insult to injury, I work in a lab where I help students with assignments. All of her students come in to their lab experience without knowing the basics of how to do the writing assignment. There is a department-wide standard for writing assignments, yet her students are allowed to skip it because this professor has "a different way of doing things." All of the adjuncts in this lab know that this full-time, tenured faculty is not teaching her students according to course and department standards, and she is getting away with it because she is tenured.

Number "5" in my introductory list to this chapter included a comment about listing the name of the professor on the course schedule next to the course a professor is teaching. That way, a student can see who is teaching a course when they register. Most of you know that when you are scheduling a class, you can choose a class based on the day, time, and professor. Many students like certain teachers and seek them out when scheduling classes. I have students ask me, "What classes will you be teaching next quarter? I loved your class and would love to sign up for your next course." Of course, I have no idea what classes I will be assigned next quarter so I can't answer that. Even after I have been assigned a class, my name is not immediately added to the course lists. Because adjuncts teach most of the classes, TBD (to be determined) is listed throughout the schedule. Students sometimes connect with a certain teacher, or seek to take or avoid a class taught by a specific person. Some of my students would like to take another class from me, but can't find my name anywhere on the course listings. Even after I have been assigned a class early in the process, my name is not added in the age of digital updates. So students who are seeking me out as an instructor cannot find which classes I am teaching. This has an adverse effect on intellectual life at the college. Students are not able to develop relationships with professors long-term, nor can they feel like they are being mentored for more than 15 weeks. Of course, it would be awkward if students were choosing an adjunct's section over a tenured faculty.

Another adjunct confided to me that she suspects it would be a mark against the full-timers if an adjuncts class filled up before a full timers when they get the prime class times. She thinks the department intentionally won't put our names beside the classes we are scheduled to teach. I am not sure that I buy into that conspiracy. I just think we are totally forgotten. I do, however, feel that it is just one of the many ways adjuncts are marginalized. As you can see by my friend's attitude concerning the conspiracy, these actions pit adjuncts against their colleagues in an unhealthy way.

Large, state-funded schools are notorious for putting research professors in charge of classes that they cannot teach. Concerned only with their own research, and out of touch with the introductory-level classes in their discipline, they have no incentive to be a good teacher. Although many know the material, they cannot explain, define or clarify their terms, devise meaningful steps, or provide feedback so students can learn. Being a teacher is far different than being a topic expert. The low-paid teaching assistants (T.A's) for these professors do most of the teaching. Unfortunately, the T.A.'s at most schools do not write the tests.

As a parent of a freshman at a state school, I have heard my child complain about how the highest grade on an exam is below 75% quite often and each test must be generously curved. If I gave a test in which all my students earned a "C" or lower, I would assume I had not taught the concepts of the test. I would either change my lectures and assignments or the test, or both. My son also explained that a professor forgot to blend the easy, medium, and hardest test questions on the midterm. Instead, this teacher gave his first period class all the easy questions, medium difficulty to the noon class, and all the advanced questions to my child's class. The unfairness of that blunder would cause an adjunct to be denied a renewed teaching contract because all the students would complain! However, this professor at my son's school, is tenured.

That sums up my description of the difference between the tenured, and the great-unwashed masses, or adjuncts. There are masses of us teaching a majority of the classes, yet we aren't given the courtesy of being called "faculty," so we are the lower-ranked. It is hard for me to provide these criticisms, as I know some good, hard working, full-time, tenured faculty. However, I know just as many mediocre and poor teachers, so why are these poor performers given status, benefits, offices, and titles when better teachers are not?

Perhaps the era of tenure is over and we should re-classify faculty. Those doing research, which greatly benefits the university, could be called "research professors." Those teaching could be called, "teaching professors." It may be a break in tradition, but if you were a student you would instantly know who to ask a classroom question and who could give you research experience.

CHAPTER VI

The Competition Among Colleagues, or
If I Share My Ideas, You'll Steal My Classes.

One of the benefits of having a large, shared room for adjunct faculty to use, is the camaraderie, and intellectual stimulation. I rub shoulders with teachers from different disciplines, but we all face the same student issues. Every adjunct professor deals with cheating, plagiarism, poor attendance, and distracted students. Because I teach in an urban environment, there are many educationally unprepared students. We also deal with gangs, single parents, a huge Somalian immigrant population, crime, learning disabilities, and sometimes-monumental parking problems.

Being able to have a sense of humor while we share ideas and possible solutions to each other's problems is extremely rewarding to me. Of course, that is, if I can actually access this shared office space. As discussed previously, my key is disabled for this space every 15 weeks and for some reason someone forgot to have it renewed this semester. (It is now 4-weeks into this semester, and I still cannot access my own file drawer in this office.) I also spend time with other professors in my department while we tutor students in the Writing, or Communication Center. These adjunct professors are often teaching the same things that I am, and we learn from each other.

Things become competitive, however, for classes that are only taught maybe twice a semester. Some of these interesting courses only come your way once every few years. One usually has to rewrite all course content, lectures, power points, assignments etc., every time you are assigned one of these rare courses. After doing all this work, it is hard to hand this information over to someone else who "gets to" teach the course you worked so hard to develop. We are not expected to do this, but sometimes a newcomer asks for help developing his/her course. Ideally, one would expect a full-timer to be doing course development because they are earning the top salaries and have benefits. They have titles like "lead instructor," or "course coordinator." However, this has not been the case for all my classes at either of the 4-year, or 2-year colleges where I have served. Some of the full-timers in our department have never given me any assistance even though they are supposed to train and provide guidance to adjuncts for a specific course.

Case in point: I was assigned a class this semester, which I taught one year ago. I went to the "course shell", maintained by a lead instructor. This shell had a course syllabus, and PowerPoint's relating to the textbook, which I could use. Although I supplement these things, I use what the department provides for each course. When I arrived to teach the first class which met for 3 hours each Friday, I was shocked and embarrassed to see the students pulling out their new editions of the textbook. My book was an old edition. I was not informed of the text change, the department syllabus listed the old book, and I was using presentation software for the wrong text because that is what the lead instructor provided. After covering up my annoyance, I quickly flipped through a student's book to see what pages I wanted to have students refer to which would relate to my lecture. I later found out that another teacher in our department had had the exact same experience as I had this term! An adjunct professor should never be surprised in this way. No teacher should have to borrow a book from her student in order to give the correct readings to the class. This is beyond unprofessional!

An even tougher pill to swallow is when this same full-time professor who should be providing guidance to adjuncts, actually uses ideas from these teachers without giving them any credit. A full-timer once was in my class evaluating my teaching and he was taking copious notes. He asked me a few detailed questions, jotting down my ideas so he could use them later. I noticed that next term, he was the ONLY one assigned to teach that class! A more professional way to handle this would be to consult the adjunct saying, "I loved how you taught that section in such a unique way. Would you mind sharing that with others at our next meeting?" How nice would it be to: 1. Give an adjunct credit for a great teaching method, 2. Share good ideas among others, 3. Reward that teacher by letting them teach that course again so they could use that great idea once more!

I once was told that I would have a visitor in my class. This person was interviewing for a full-time faculty position at the liberal arts school where I was teaching a junior-level business communications class. This person was fresh out of his PhD, and had done no teaching. He had no experience in the business world and he furiously copied my lecture examples. He asked for a copy of my syllabus, which I had developed myself along with all the assignments. Of course, you know the rest of the story. The college hired him, and he was assigned that course from then on, and I never taught it again. This has happened twice to me. The second time, I was tempted to fake an appendicitis attack so I wouldn't have to train my replacement once again. Of course, I didn't, and just tried to see the bright side to the backhanded compliment.

One thing I appreciate is the occasional training sessions available at my current school. I have attended classes to learn the online grade book system and new teaching techniques, and I have attended daylong trainings for tutors. Unfortunately, some of these are only held once a year and I am often teaching on the day they are taught. Still, I feel like I am receiving the training I need. An article in The Higher Education Workplace notes that sometimes adjuncts at community colleges are trained better than 4-year institutions.[8] The article speculates that that's because two-year colleges depend so heavily on part-time faculty. One has to be self-motivated and seek out new ways to teach and adapt to new software and technology in order to truly stay relevant, however.

The problems I discussed at the beginning of this chapter have nothing to do with a lack of training. Not being given the correct textbook, being told to use a department syllabus that is out of date, and not having a working to key to a shared office is lack of proper management. If someone has the title of "coordinator" or "lead" for a course, they should make sure the information provided to adjuncts is current. Especially since they are doing essentially the same job, minus the minimal management tasks, as an adjunct professor.

If you think my tales of woe are merely one person's whining, read the blog by "The Homeless Adjunct." The economic disparities of faculty and college administrators are detailed, along with numerous ideas for reform by John A Casey Jr.

CHAPTER VII

The Reason Adjuncts Dress Like Bums
Sorry guys, It's True

I shared an office with a history adjunct at a liberal arts college for a few years. In our office there was a coat rack on which three blazers were hung. Let's say they were brown tweed, navy blue and gray. This adjunct would run in seconds before his class was starting in jeans, a T-shirt, and dirty running shoes. He would contemplate his options for one second and select a blazer to throw over his T-shirt. It was kind of fun to watch him mull over his options. Some days, based on his shirt color, none of the choices were good.

This adjunct professor had engaging lectures, but obviously spent little time in prepping details like a schedule, tests and course expectations. I noticed over a year's time, he didn't even bother to ensure that the T-shirts he wore were void of lettering and advertisements. This made for a really funny look. Peeking from the center of his chest beneath a preppy blazer were a few letters from a word, or a curious partial image. This was either a distraction or a way to keep students focused and guessing.

Occasionally I would tease him about his blazer selection and one day he told me he had another job to make ends meet and he barely had time to get to his classes. He also said, he didn't feel like investing in a wardrobe, because the school "hadn't invested in him." Of course, not all unprofessional wardrobes are caused by adjuncts having to work other jobs. Most adjunct professors probably don't consciously choose to dress unprofessionally out of protest for their lack of status or respect. I do wonder, does an adjunct professor who isn't dressed like a full-time professional, reinforce the less-than status?

Robert Weissberg, Professor of Political Science, Emeritus at the University of Illinois-Urbana, commented on the importance of dressing professionally in the classroom.[9] In his opinion, we are culturally conditioned to defer to those who dress professionally. He alluded to the diminished social authority of professors because of their casual attire. Of course, my friend who comes straight from the hospital where she works as a nurse to teach a course during her lunch hour can't change her clothes before class. She teaches in her scrubs. The strapped-for-cash adjuncts who ride their bikes to work need to be dressed casually for their commute. Weissberg joked at the end of his article that professors should be given a wardrobe and grooming stipend to help them stay professional. Most adjuncts, however, would settle for a living wage and clothing is the least of their worries.

The reason I decided to include this chapter is because I think that dressing too casually leads to less respect from administrators and students. Getting little respect from one's boss and students gives a teacher little reason to take pride in their job, making it less likely they will invest in a teaching wardrobe. It seems like a vicious circle, but it starts with the administration. If they called an adjunct an "adjunct professor"; if they paid them a little better; and if they set an example themselves, then perhaps they would see a change in the appearance of the 80% who are teaching our college students.

Of course, there are those who dress casually because they just want to. They don't see the relevance to teaching in an "artificial uniform." A few years ago I became aware of how important this issue is. I accidentally performed a perception exercise with one of my classes, which proved it DOES matter how I dress. It was spring break of 2009. My husband and I had taken our boys to the Big Island, Hawaii and taught them to surf. We had driven to Chicago to save on airfare and the return trip was going to be $600.00 cheaper if we returned one day before I would start teaching. I knew my return trip would be cutting things close, so I had packed my briefcase and set out clothes for my first day teaching in advance. Everything was ready for a quick few hours of sleep to shake off the jet lag before teaching.

Things didn't go as planned when one of our planes was late. We were driving from Chicago with barely enough time for me to get to my first class. When we pulled up to the house, I grabbed my briefcase, and jumped into the car without changing my attire. This class only met once a week and I had a lot planned for the first day. I needed to get through one chapter after all the course preliminaries, so I hit the ground running. I gave the class something to work on with a partner after 2 hours of lecture, and then I took a moment to look down at my feet. I had cut my feet on some corral and wearing shoes was painful. I was wearing flip flops with butterfly bandages on my tanned feet. Above my nearly bare feet I wore jeans and a T-shirt. To top things off, I had slept in the airport, hadn't washed my face, and my hair was a bit wild.

Before class ended, I asked what the students thought the course was going to be like after their first day. One student gushed, "This class is going to be so great, because you are SOOO laid back." Knowing why he thought this, I asked, "What makes you think that?" Of course, the students commented that I was dressed casually so they thought the class would be fun. I then told me I had a rough return trip and they could never expect to see me looking that way again. I said, "Sure, we will have fun. But I want you to take this class seriously. I expected timely, accurate work."

Students do notice our attire. Some teachers know this is true but they pretend it doesn't matter. Those who know it matters may be trying to change the shallow way society relies on the exterior. Sure, over time a mature person will look past a person's appearance; most students, however, won't. As an adjunct professor, I don't want to have to work twice as hard to overcome some stereotype about my teaching based on how I've dressed.

All this discussion of adjunct's dressing either sloppily or well really is trivial compared to the topic in my next chapter.

CHAPTER VIII

Safety Issues and Blood in the Hallway or,
Should I Risk My Life for This?

Virginia Tech, Santa Monica College, New River Community College, and Lone Star College. What do these schools have in common? Of course, everyone knows about the Virginia Tech shootings in 2007 where 32 people were killed. The other 3 colleges listed are community colleges where fatal shootings have occurred so far in 2013. We all know that anywhere large numbers of people are gathered, the potential for violence exists. It is hard to monitor large numbers of people. However, community colleges where there are a higher percentage of adjunct professors than most four-year schools, seem to target more violence than other colleges.

"Our students go home at night and we don't know what they are doing at home, but they can still bring issues back to campus with them," says Gary Lyle, chief of the Department of Public Safety at Anne Arundel Community College (AACC) in Maryland. "At a four-year school their roommates might alert people to issues."[10] Ann McClure's interview at Arundel seems to be true. A commuter campus is very difficult to monitor. With these dangers in mind, an adjunct at a two-year college has a lot of safety issues to consider.

I never saw anyone be arrested while I taught at three different four-year colleges. Of course, students are arrested all the time at these schools, it just didn't happen as often as it does at the community college where I teach. I once had four police officers come to surprise one of my students and arrest him in class. I wasn't informed ahead of time and it was quite a shock to my students. Needless to say, I didn't get a lot of teaching done that hour!

Last semester a man was stabbed, and ran into the building where I was teaching. He was bleeding profusely in a bathroom near the room where I lectured. The wide trail of blood into the building was shocking. A student interrupted him as he was removing his shirt and bleeding into a bathroom sink. The student offered to help him, but he declined. We were never sure if this was due to foggy thinking and blood loss, or a fear police involvement due to illegal activity. Someone had already called the police when she saw the massive trail of blood striping the hallway. When I became aware of the situation, I locked my door and tried to continue teaching. I didn't know if the victim's stabber was on his way to finish him off. I didn't know if we were supposed to be on lock-down or not.

I received an e-mail saying that my floor was now a crime scene, but that I should continue to teach my next class on the third floor. I went to security with the student who found the victim in the bathroom. This student who found the victim in the bathroom had to give a statement to the police. As I was walking up the stairs to the third floor to teach, I had to pass the trail of gore going to the second floor. The door to the bathroom was propped open in full view of the open staircase. I spent a lot of time that afternoon trying to answer student questions. I didn't have any answers for them.

Working in an urban environment increases risks of all types. I wish that some message would have been sent from someone with authority praising all of us teaching on the second floor for keeping our heads, and soldiering on. I wish that I didn't feel professionally and personally expendable in my adjunct position.

Tenured and temporary professors alike share these dangers. However, a full-timer has disability insurance and sick leave if they need it to cope with these events, and an adjunct professor is granted none of those things.

Every few years I have a difficult student who is mentally ill. An estimated 26.2 percent of Americans ages 18 and older—about one in four adults—suffer from a diagnosable mental disorder in a given year. The Archives of General Psychiatry published this information based on a survey in 2005.[11] I hope the numbers have not increased, but I am sure they have not gone down. If one fourth of all adults are mentally ill, you can bet we will be teaching many of them. Community colleges, with their low barrier to entry, have an even higher number of mentally ill students on their campuses. Because more teachers at a community college are adjuncts, it is the adjuncts that have a more dangerous and difficult population to teach.

I have had students throw things, curse, storm out of class and stalk me and others in the class. Again, this is just a part of teaching in a large public system. However, if adjuncts were given the support and respect they needed in these situations, it would be easier to tolerate. Being physically fit and aware of my environment helps me face these situations. Being strong enough not to change a grade when bullied is sometimes not enough. A little clout, and perhaps more pay would help an adjunct professor feel it is worth it.

I have to admit, after that stabbing victim was near the room where I was teaching, I did a bit of soul searching. Was the sometimes satisfying teaching experience really worth it?

CHAPTER IX

Full Disclosure; I'm Great at This But Not
Making Any More Than When I Sucked.

I have been evaluated only three times by a lead instructor (full-timer) over the course of 15 years of college teaching. I'm not complaining. I'm glad I am trusted to do a good job. However, a helpful teaching evaluation can give a good teacher additional ideas, and make them feel like someone likes what they are doing. One of my evaluations was specifically helpful. I talked through an assignment I had created with this lead instructor. She helped me see how to use my time more efficiently and I appreciated her feedback.

Most professors, however, only receive evaluations from their students, not other experienced teachers. At least one of my classes fills out a course evaluation every single term. Some students like to learn, are expecting academic rigor, and give honest feedback. Unfortunately, a lot of students are used to grade inflation, have a hard time meeting expectations, and give dishonest, overly negative feedback. I have never had terribly negative evaluations. My students know that I genuinely like them, but that I am scrupulously fair in my grading. Unfortunately, some teachers cave to the students' demands for higher grades knowing that negative student evaluations may result in their not being asked back for the next term. There needs to be a better system for evaluating professors in order to prevent grade inflation.

Relying solely on students' ratings of professors is like asking restaurants to rate their health inspector! Some students and restaurants may resent being graded at all and they will not give reasonable, honest reports of their teacher/inspector's abilities. I can see some café owners thanking a health inspector for helping them find that refrigerator that needed maintenance. I'm sure this doesn't happen very often, though. Of course, I have students who thanked me for grading them in a way that taught them to write or think more clearly. Again, this does not happen often, and it takes a mature student to give honest, positive evaluations while earning poor grade in a class.

An even more inaccurate evaluation tool exists on ratemyprofessor.com. This online tool allows students to post their impressions of teachers online. It also allows you to rate your professor's hotness with a chili pepper icon! I have to admit, I look at my own press on occasion. The problem with these voluntary evaluations is they are mostly going to be negative by default. Would you take the effort to go to a website, find the instructor, and post a comment if your class experience was good or positive? Most people would not go to the effort unless they were upset and looking for a place to vent. I am impressed when someone actually takes the time to thank me for my teaching, but most do it in person, not online.

So, it is clear that both adjunct and tenured or full-time professors are not accurately rated based on their abilities to teach. (See the previous chapter's discussion of tenured faculty who seems to be mentally unstable.) No one charts how much students have learned, or how diverse learning styles are accommodated. So how do administrators decide what to pay an employee? Is a teacher's pay based on years of experience? Unfortunately, from an adjunct professor's point of view, no.

The college where I currently teach pays adjuncts by the class and the number of times that class meets. If someone were to be hired right now, new, having no prior teaching experience, they would be paid the same as me. Even my 15-years of college teaching experience will not increase that per-class amount.

According to many many state calculations, adjuncts' pay increases have not kept pace with either full-faculty or inflation. An interesting read on this subject is an essay titled, "Adjunct Pay: More Experience Means Less Money," by Ellen Balleisen.[12] By her calculations, an adjunct teaching in the New York City area now makes $2.07 per contact hour LESS than they did in 2002!

When I first started teaching I was not nearly as confident as I am now. I was more likely to give a domineering, loud student the benefit of the doubt on certain essay questions, just to keep them from complaining. I didn't read the Wall Street Journal daily and use real-life applications in class like I do today. I was not nearly as good as I am now at grading student work, putting together engaging lectures and case studies, and creating good tests. I'm much better now, but this experience has not paid off financially. If the studies of inflation and increased cost of living are correct, I am now making LESS than when I was inexperienced.

A program on National Public Radio, September 22, 2013, featured a story about a very popular adjunct professor, Margaret Mary Votjkov.[13] After 25 years of teaching French at Duquesne, the university had not renewed her contract. As a part-time professor, she had been earning about $10,000 a year, and had no health insurance. As an aside, she was making more per class than I currently do. Her contract was not renewed, not because she wasn't a good teacher, but because it had become hard for her to teach a full schedule when she was diagnosed with cancer. She died homeless. After her death, the outcry earned her a news story and some radio time, but as far as I can research, nothing changed for the adjuncts at that school.

Again, people at my school are making less than her and living with no insurance. Some donate plasma for money or ride their bikes to school to save transportation costs. Most can't afford the cafeteria food and pack their lunches daily. Many of my colleagues cannot afford to travel to see family during the holidays.

Adjuncts at my college are not motivated by money, or they would be working elsewhere. I benefit from being a self-motivated person. That is probably why I have driven myself to become a better and better teacher. But what about professors who aren't so motivated? I'm afraid their students suffer. As a tutor, I deal with students who are not being taught the basics in class. They come to me not knowing rudimentary things, not because they have trouble learning. These students have fallen victim to lazy teachers who know that what they do in the classroom will not be noticed, and if they work harder to improve, their bank account will never know the difference.

Let's be clear. I am not asking for a pay raise. Colleges and Universities have felt the pinch of decreased federal and state funding. I merely want my pay to reflect rises in the cost of living and to reflect the increases given to full-time faculty. And, of course, it would be nice to have a system that rewards me for doing a better job than when I first started out.

CHAPTER X

Trying to make a difference, being threatened by your
boss for it,
And yes, I have his threats in writing!

My husband has encouraged me to do something
besides adjunct teaching for years now. He remembers me
as the woman who worked in human resources, who was
a consultant, and broke sales records in office equipment
marketing. He liked seeing me in the social circle of success
and respect, and he never saw my self-esteem trampled
the way it sometimes is now. I agree that in some of my
previous jobs my efforts were rewarded, especially when
I went above a measured standard; broke a sales goal,
or conducted well-run meeting. As discussed earlier, no
one sees or measures one's great teaching moments. No
one is there when a frustrated student suddenly smiles,
and understands something for the first time. The time I
spend going over poor assignments with a student giving
them extra examples until they can see errors seems to go
unnoticed. The detailed rubrics I create in order to have
a fair standard for every assignment are only admired
by other adjuncts. The weekends and holidays when I
answer students' questions via e-mail are never rewarded.

However, I do love what I do. I am intellectually stimulated and challenged. I am surrounded by so much diversity and culture and youthful energy, that I miss it when I am not teaching. I have seen 50 year-olds who have been laid off come back to college and love every minute of it. A bitter student from Alaska who "hated the lower 48 states" grew to love the Midwest when she made friends in my class. I saw a rose bloom beneath her piercings and tattoos and her academic growth was miraculous.

I am in good company. The 2nd lady, Dr. Jill Biden, has been a professor at Northern Virginia Community College for several years and she's taught in a college setting for three decades.[14] She and I have both had students come to us for counseling. We both have had students being pushed into arranged marriages, and we have tried to listen to them. We both have had students write papers describing physical abuse. And we both feel like we are making a difference in the lives of college students.

Last year, one of my former students contacted me. I remembered her as a shy girl. A refugee from Sierra Leone, she was adapting to the cold winter when she was in my class. At that time, I never saw her in class without her coat, hat, and scarf on. She e-mailed me, asking if I remembered her. Of course I did. She stood out among the other students. This girl wanted to know if I would help her write her Valedictorian speech for graduation. It was an honor to help her. Cases like this keep me teaching in a system that rewards mediocrity, and penalizes those who try to change things for the better.

Let me describe how this happened recently. It was the first day of the first semester. Syllabus in hand, ready to quickly memorize the names of all my students before the second class meeting, I walked from the parking garage to class. I happened to call our department assistant on my cell phone as I was walking. She said, "Oh, by the way the class you're going to now at 11:00 has been given to (full-timer). I stopped walking in the middle of the street. "What?" She continued, "(full timer) was accidentally assigned two classes at 9 AM today and since he couldn't be in two places at once, we gave him your 11:00 class and you're going to teach the 9 AM." Fortunately for me, it was the same course that I had planned to teach, so the syllabus and course content would be similar. Of course, that meant that I had already missed the first day of class because I didn't know I was to teach at 9 AM. I could not comprehend how (full timer) did not know he was scheduled to teach two 9 AM classes. One has to have syllabi prepared in advance for each class on the first day. How could he have a syllabus prepared for the class if he hadn't looked at what time it was meeting? Of course, I knew the answer to that. Some tenured faculty were allowed by the department chair to develop lazy habits. They wander into class with no syllabus, no real plan for the semester, and wing it. I'm not sure if that is what happened this time, but I've heard of other faculty doing this.

Saying a prayer that I would remain professional, I walked to the 11:00 class that was no longer mine. I greeted the class. I then said that although I was originally going to be their teacher, another teacher had been double-booked and he was on his way. I reassured them that the class location would remain the same. 5 minutes late (full timer) walked in. I asked him if he had explained to the 9 AM class that another teacher would be assigned.

He said he couldn't really because he had to attend to his "real" 9 AM class.

My e-mail was added to the 9 AM course list later that day. I received 20 e-mails asking where I was, if the class location was changed, and if they could (ha ha) give me a bad evaluation for my no-show. After professionally responding to the e-mails, I started teaching one day behind. The class went well, the students were great people, and it ended on a positive note.

I can't help asking what if I had taken a job teaching a 9 AM class at the business school next door. Many of us piece together classes at both schools. It was just assumed that I would be available to take the 9 AM without asking me!

I finally got the courage to talk to my boss about this and a few other incidents. I followed up by putting my concerns in an e-mail so there was a formal document listing these concerns. I shared these concerns with no one else. I didn't gossip about the department's lack of professionalism, or complain to his boss, the Dean. I wanted to professionally discuss ways to prevent these catastrophes from happening to me again.

His response was shocking and curt. To summarize, his first e-mail stated that I was being considered for a Tuesday Thursday class which was one of the rare, popular ones to teach. However, he continued, after going over my criticisms in the e-mail, I was no longer being considered. Later he followed with an e-mail stating that, "I can always reassign your Friday class." Here he threatened to take away a class that I had spent a month preparing. Of course, he was foolish enough to make these threats in writing.

After settling in to the semester, I decided to try to make things better, even if I lost my job. I shared his threats and my concerns about general unprofessional behavior with his boss, the Dean. She happens to be a friend, and I taught under her when she was my Department Chair years ago. She was shocked, but quiet and brooding after our talk. She said she would, "See what she could do." It turns out, she is an interim Dean, and she is not being interviewed for the permanent position, although she has held it for 2 years. When I asked why she wasn't being considered, she said, "I don't have a PhD." She had done a great job for 2 years, yet she was not being considered. She didn't think she would be able to help me because she didn't have longevity or clout.

Once again, academic tradition was causing a system failure. This system has proven to lead to laziness among full-time instructors, and abuse from department chairs. It seems that I don't have any recourse and my attempts to make things more professional were in vain. However, this text will prove whether the pen is mightier than the flawed system.

Writing this when I have no firm teaching contract for next semester will be nailing my coffin at my current school, I know. I don't expect to receive a contract after shedding the light on these issues. Like others before me, I am trying to take the high road. In Isaac Sweeney's article, "Why I Should Keep My Mouth Shut," he stated, "I had heard horror stories of adjuncts losing their contracts because they spoke out against the system that devalues them (not to mention their students), but I guess I thought I was invincible. I must admit there's a little part of me that feels proud that I took the risk."[15] His well-presented criticisms of the system was published by

<u>The Chronicle</u>, and James Madison University as well as the Blue Ridge Community college suddenly decided not to have him teach classes anymore. His well thought-out article was published and praised. Usually publishing increases a professor's standing in the academic world. However, when his work shined the light of truth on a faulty system of educating college students, he was vilified.

I hope the same doesn't happen to me, but I am not afraid of the consequences. I've already begun to reinvent myself and prepare for a new career. I admit, it would be nice to keep teaching college students in some capacity. More importantly though, I hope this writing opens up a dialogue about the way college students are being taught. My desire is that every student would have a well-trained, motivated instructor who feels valuable to their college.

[1] Audrey June, "Adjuncts build Strength in Numbers", Chronicle of Higher Education. November 5, 2012

[2] Tyler Kinkade "AAUP, Don't Cut Adjunct Hours To Avoid Obama Care Requirements" Huffington Post, 4/4/2013

[3] *Stuart Rojstaczer, &, Christopher Healy,"Grading in American Colleges and Universities",Teachers College Record,* Date Published: March 04, 2010 http://www.tcrecord.org ID Number: 15928, Date Accessed: 3/4/2010 1:46:08 PM

[4] Alysia Filey, "The Real Reason College Costs so Much" Wall Street Journal, August, 24-24, 2013.

[5] Institute for College Access & Success, "Quick Facts about Financial Aid and Community Colleges, 2007-2008" May 2009, http://www.ticas.org/files/pub/cc_fact_sheet.pdf

[6] Sarah Kendzior, Phd. "Academia's Indentured Servants." MMT Site. April, 13, 2013 http://mikenormaneconomics.blogspot.com/2013/04/sarah-kendzior-academias-indentured.html

[7] The Truth About Tenure in Higher Education *Published by the Higher Education Departments of the National Education Association and the American Federation of Teachers.NEA. org 2013*

[8] "Adjunct Professors Often Lack Training in How to Handle Disabilities in the Classroom, Experts Say" *The Higher Education Workplace* W i n t e r 2 011-12

[9] Robert Weissberg, "Professors Should Dress Like Professionals" <u>Minding the Campus,</u> April 4, 2011.

[10] Ann McClure, "Strategies for Managing Security Issues at Two-Year Institutions," <u>University Business,</u> <u>Jul 2009</u>

[11] Kessler RC, Chiu WT, Demler O, Walters EE. Prevalence, severity, and comorbidity of twelve-month DSM-IV disorders in the National Comorbidity Survey Replication (NCS-R). *Archives of General Psychiatry,* 2005 Jun;62(6):617-27.

[12] Ellen Balleisen, "Adjunct Pay: More Experience Means Less Money," <u>http://cunyadjunctproject.org/</u> <u>files/2009/10/balleisen-in-advocate.pdf</u>

[13] Claudio Sanchez, "The Sad Death Of An Adjunct Professor Sparks A Labor Debate" National Public Radio Broadcast September 22, 2013 7:37 AM

[14] Wayne Goodwyn's interview Jill Biden, NRP weekend edition, Sunday, September 1, 2013.

[15] Isaac Sweeney, "Why I Should Keep My Mouth Shut" March 16, 2011, The Chronicle of Higher Education